Exploring
ALFRISTON
and
THE CUCKMERE VALLEY

Sandy Hernu

S.B. Publications

First published in 1992 by S.B. Publications
C/o 19 Grove Road, Seaford, East Sussex BN25 1TP.

Reprinted 1993
Revised and Reprinted 1996
© Copyright 1992 Sandy Hernu

ISBN **1 85770 014 7**

All rights reserved. No part of this publication may be reproduced, stored in a retrieval system, or transmitted, in any form or by any means, electronic, mechanical, photocopying, recording or otherwise without the prior permission of the publishers.

Typeset, printed and bound by
MFP Design & Print
Tel: 0161 864 4540.

By the same author:
East Sussex Walks (Brighton, Lewes and Eastbourne)
East Sussex Walks (In and around the Rural Villages)
East Sussex Walks (Exploring 1066 Country)
Secrets of East Sussex

CONTENTS

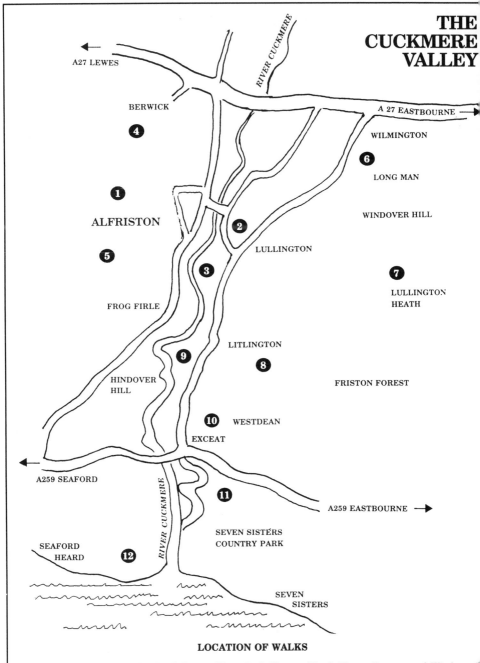

THE CUCKMERE VALLEY

A27 LEWES

RIVER CUCKMERE

A 27 EASTBOURNE

BERWICK

WILMINGTON

LONG MAN

ALFRISTON

WINDOVER HILL

LULLINGTON

FROG FIRLE

LULLINGTON HEATH

LITLINGTON

FRISTON FOREST

HINDOVER HILL

WESTDEAN

EXCEAT

A259 SEAFORD

RIVER CUCKMERE

A259 EASTBOURNE

SEVEN SISTERS COUNTRY PARK

SEAFORD HEARD

SEVEN SISTERS

LOCATION OF WALKS

1. Alfriston, Roman Road The South Downs Way
2. Lullington Church and Long Bridge
3. Alfriston to Litlington
4. Winton Street to Berwick Church
5. France Bottom
6. Wilmington and The Long Man
7. Lullington Heath Nature Reserve and Windover
8. Litlington, Friston Forest and Charleston Manor
9. Litlington, The River and The White Horse
10. Exceat and Westdean
11. The Seven Sisters Country Park
12. Cuckmere Haven

INTRODUCTION

Much of the busy A27 between Lewes and Eastbourne stretches alongside the bare and beautiful South Downs. These downs give way to a valley at, what is known locally as, "Drusilla's roundabout". Pause for a while in your journey. Pause and follow the sign that says "Alfriston 1½ miles". Here in the Cuckmere Valley you will find everything that represents our childish dreams of the countryside. From rambling roses clambering round cottage doorways, to the handful of flint villages nestling by the river. An abundance of wild flowers strewn across downland walks and in the distance, the sea. Here, the white chalk cliffs are sheer and provide a sharp contrast as they rise steeply to meet the sky.

In Alfriston, the largest village, you can see buildings dating from the fourteenth century onwards, all beautifully preserved and jostling for a position around the old Market Cross. You can wander past the heavily beamed Star Inn and its counterpart, the George on the opposite side of the road, then make your way through the Twitten to the Tye (or village green). Here you will find St. Andrew's Church. The Cathedral of the Downs as it is called is splendidly sited by the meandering Cuckmere river, which boasts some of the most delightful walks before it finally reaches the sea, three miles further on. This enchanting river is then closely guarded by the gently rolling downs, whose lower slopes turn gold with corn in the summer and the long umber shadows that pervade them, provide an everchanging aspect to delight the beholder. This following description of the area, echoes some of my sentiments. It is from a Sussex newspaper dated September 1783.

"It is only three miles from Seaford. I was never in so mountainous a country in my life. Go where you will and you are still surrounded by hills and mountains and what is extraordinary to me, the whole is in a state of cultivation; in some places corn, in other turnips, potatoes and all kinds of vegetables, without even a wall or partition to be seen. The variegated colours of the earth have an amazing pleasing effect. Those who have sheep have shepherds to keep them to their own ground.

I rode yesterday over these hills, upon the top of which, when I looked down, it made my head giddy with delight".

Villages steeped in history and a valley that goes back into the mists of time. Come with me, let's explore it.

Traffic in Alfriston, c.1900

ALFRISTON
Dene Car Park

When you reach Alfriston, leave your car in one of the two car parks. Alfriston has to be seen on foot. Then you can absorb the atmosphere of this downland village and its surroundings and gaze at your leisure at the lovely old buildings.

Let's start this leisurely exploration of Alfriston in the far corner of Dene Car Park. Behind a flint wall and an iron gate is the old 15th century Forge, now sensitively converted into holiday accommodation. Prior to this it had been run as a Blacksmith's Museum and village Heritage Centre. It closed as a working forge in 1930 and the blacksmith then re-established his smithy in a couple of barns, almost opposite. This complex has also been converted and is confusingly called The Forge as well. Three handsome Georgian fronted houses lie beyond these barns. The last and the largest, Tuckvar, supposedly has its fair share of ghostly connections.

As we leave the Old Forge, glance to the left and notice the conical flint tower. It was built about 1800. During this time, the Duke of Wellington had his troops stationed in Alfriston, owing to the threat of an invasion by the French. In fact, the very Car Park you are standing in was a parade ground for those soldiers. The flint tower however, is of uncertain origins. Some say it was a shot tower, the openings being for lighting and relining the furnace. Some say it was a lock-up, there are several others, similar in this country. On the map of 1873, it's marked as dovecote. Other suggestions include, a gunstore or something to do with the brick kilns that were once sited down the road. Incidentally, North Street which separates the two Car Parks used to be called "Down the Bricks".

The Flint Tower

North Street

On leaving the car park by the east exit, look to your left again and notice the very fine example of a Queen Anne house. Many, many years ago it used to sell beer. Now, where the brewery used to be, is a rose garden.

As you turn right up North Street you will notice a single storey shed type structure. This supposedly was an old Victorian cabbies shelter, once placed outside Victoria Station. The row of red brick Edwardian houses beyond, contrast rather sharply with the mellow properties on the opposite side of the road. These cottages, with only the pavement as a frontage, used to be the local workhouse.

Badgers restaurant was formerly known as The Urn. Prior to 1930 it was a bakery and in 1801 it was a meeting place for dissentors from St. Andrew's church.

On the opposite corner is Bank House, with a long gently sloping roof, this is known as a "cat's slide" roof. Tucked away just beyond Bank House is a low ceilinged premises, originally a glove factory.

The leather for the glove factory was obtained from a tannery sited between the river and the High Street behind the George Inn. A house called The Tanneries now marks the original area.

North Street, c. 1930

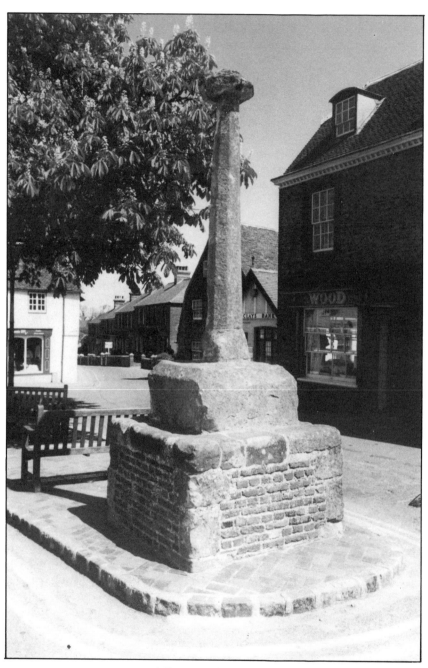

The Market Cross

The Village Square

Arriving in the Village Square, or Waterloo Square as it was called, the first thing that meets our eyes is the old Market Cross. This was erected during the reign of Henry IV, when Alfriston was granted the right to hold a weekly market. The idea of a market cross, and this one indeed did then have a cross on it, was to ensure "all those that traded in its shadows, traded honestly and fairly".

The weekly market held in the fifteenth or sixteenth century was the highlight of the week for the inhabitants of the valley. A social occasion where they could sell their produce, buy or barter. Two hundred years later the Duke of Wellington's uniformed troops thronged around the cross, poised to fight a war. At the end of the nineteenth century the Eastbourne Foxhounds would meet here for the Sunday hunt, horses pawing the ground, restless with anticipation of the forthcoming event.

The little row of cottages that form the north side of the square had soldiers billeted in them in 1800. They were also used as a Quartermaster's Stores. Now they are shops, tempting the many visitors to Alfriston with gifts, clothes, cream teas and magazines. It is interesting to learn, that the first London newspaper to be sold in the village was the Daily Mail on May 4th 1896. Until then only Sussex papers were available.

On your right as you look down the High Street, is the lovely Georgian, bow-windowed village store. It has been a grocers for over a hundred years and at the turn of the century was owned by a gentleman possessing the magnificent name of Ebenezer Comfort. It was during his ownership that the galleried floor, which you can still see today, was open to the public selling drapery and hardware items. "Sally's" Craft and Gift Shop, the other side of the village store used to be the old Police Station. Before 1931 it was the Chapel House or Manse.

The Chestnut tree in the centre of the square was planted to commemorate Queen Victoria's accession to the throne. Recently, in the hopes of prolonging its life, the chestnut has had to be severely pruned and no longer looks so prolific. The Market Cross is also somewhat different to its original structure. Around 1830, the rather peculiar 'mushroom' replaced the old cross on the top. Gone too are the three ancient stone steps that surrounded it. Instead, there is a brick base. In 1955, a lorry crashed into the cross causing extensive damage and although skillfully repaired, the new shaft is a great deal shorter.

Market Cross and Village Square, c.1890

Entering Alfriston from the south, c.1890

Next to the village store is the Smugglers Inn, formerly Market Cross House. It claimed to have, at one time, 48 doors, 21 rooms and 6 staircases. The infamous smuggler, Stanton Collins, spent a number of years here, before the law finally caught him and sentenced him to "seven years penal servitude in one of the colonies". When he finally returned to this country he made his home in Worthing, where he is now buried.

Edwardian Alfriston

Saddlers, c.1930

"Saddlers Tearooms" beyond, was, as its name indicates occupied by a saddler and harness maker. It has been a teashop for about fifty years and in addition has sold a variety of goods such as sweets, postcards, gifts, films, dairy products, tyres, engineering accessories and even petrol. The petrol pump was sited in the tiny front garden. Apparently, the old petrol tank still exists under the teashop floor.

Opposite the village stores you will find the handsome Cross House which, until recently, was Wood's the butchers (see front cover illustration). The Wood family had been butchers in Alfriston since 1886; their first shop being part of the lovely old Manor Farm House on the adjacent corner. In 1910 they moved into Cross House. River Lane, that separates these two properties, was known as "Slaughter House Lane". The barns at the end being the slaughter houses for the butcher's shop. Prior to 1910, Cross House was owned by a Mr. Pierce who was a Fly proprietor. "What is that" you may ask? A Fly proprietor delivers goods or massages as speedily as possible, by means of a horse or horse and cart. He must have been a busy man in the days before telephones, transport or fax machines.

The Star Inn, c.1912

The Star Inn today

The High Street

Walking down the high street we come to the Star Inn. Opposite is the George Inn and the Tudor House restaurant. These three properties were built at the end of the fourteenth century. The Star was originally used as a resting place for pilgrims when visiting the shrine of St. Richard at Chichester. There seems to be some uncertainty as to when it actually became an inn. It is a beautifully preserved example of a pre-Tudor building, its interior even more heavily beamed than the exterior. It is interesting to note, that the exterior beams were once covered with plaster and it was at the turn of this century that they were exposed and cleaned. Note too, the red painted figurehead on the corner of Star Lane. This came from a Dutch ship, wrecked near Cuckmere Haven in the 17th century. Now look up and see the unusual carvings and the Horsham stone roof. Supposedly each slab weighs half a hundredweight.

The George Inn, initially a house or perhaps even two, was later a coaching inn. The old coaching archway was at the southern end of it, now converted to form part of the existing property. Apart from partially being an inn, the George was home to a variety of trades, including a barber's shop, butcher's yard and a garage.

The 14th-century Tudor House next door, looks a great deal younger. The large, almost street level windows, unfortunately give it a modern appearance. The windows were put in after the first World War, when it was trading as a grocers. A smuggler's bolthole used to connect it to the George. Look across the road now to "Steamer Trading Cookshop" and "Magpie Books and Gifts". These two shops were all a part of the jettied "Steamer Inn". At the end of the nineteenth century, a local man called Mr. Bodle, bought the property and opened "Bodle's Dairy", which traded in Alfriston for a number of years.

Meanwhile, a relative of Mr. Bodle, thought to try his luck a little further afield. He emigrated to New Zealand, which he found very much to his liking. He purchased some land, built himself a home and renamed the area Alfriston, New Zealand. He then erected a church, an inn, a village store and a number of houses, bearing a strong resemblance in layout to the English Alfriston we know. Alfriston, New Zealand still exists today and is a thriving community.

Further on we pass the United Reformed Church, built in 1801. Next to it is a lane, known locally as a "twytten". This leads on to the Tye. Twytten House, on the corner, has been an antique shop for a number of years and before that it was a paint shop. Opposite, you have the old Farmhouse, thought to be of the oldest buildings in Alfriston.

The Wingrove, c.1890

Deans Place Hotel

Now, we come to The Apiary, a large craft and gift shop. Historian, Florence Pagden lived there. She wrote a charming little book about her recollections of Alfriston which, as she implies in the preface, was started in 1895 and finished in 1950. Her father, which the name "Apiary" suggests, kept bees. He too, wrote a book entitled "£70 a year. How I make it, by my bees".

The long low diamond-paned building we are outside now, is Moonrakers restaurant. It once belonged to a peruke or wig maker and later was a cottage known as Two Ways. Next to it is a large shop, at one time a fine old coach house. Beyond that are the cottages converted from the stables belonging to the Wingrove.

We have passed, on this walk down the High Street, other properties, such as The Chestnut Tearooms, Lavendar Cottage, Southdown House and several more. All have history of some sort attached to them, but I think you the reader and onlooker have enough information to enable you to capture a colourful and fairly accurate picture of Alfriston in an era long since gone.

The Wingrove Inn faces due south and seems to mark the end of the high street. This impressive, colonial type house was built in 1870 by a Mr. Porter as a private residence with racing stables to the rear. Mr. Porter, his wife and family, lived at the Wingrove for about twenty years. It was a very successful racing stables, so it seems ironic, that when out of kindness, Mr. Porter stood surety for a friend's debts, it proved to be his downfall and he lost everything, including the Wingrove. In 1898, it was sold to a Harry Batho, also a racehorse owner. In 1912, his horse, Longset won the Lincoln. However, even when Longset won the Lincoln, history seemed determined to repeat itself. A Mr Albert Morgan, fishmonger and bookmaker from Seaford, came to Alfriston once a week, selling fresh fish from his barrow. He also took all the local bets on Longset, convinced it couldn't possibly win the Lincoln, which would of course, enable him to make a fortune. Longset won and Mr. Morgan, like Mr. Porter, lost everything including his home, Albion House at South Street in Seaford.

At the southerly end of the village, situated in the most delightful gardens, is Deans Place Hotel. The original building was a moated manor house and owned, during the reign of Elizabeth I by the de Dene family. The name de Dene appears on records as far back as 1355. Deans Place seems to have its fair quota of ghost stories. The most popular one being of a lady in blue who would tap on the door, walk in and then vanish into thin air. Some years ago, during extensive alterations to the building, a skeleton was discovered. Since then, the lady in blue has disappeared, and has never been seen again.

St. Andrew's Church

The Clergy House

The Tye

On reaching the Tye you will find a number of pleasing aspects of Alfriston surrounding you. To the south there is the winding river, meadows and trees, the downs providing a varied green backcloth. To the west, there is an assortment of old terracotta-tiled roofs and flowered gardens, making up the rear approaches of the high street properties. To the north, is the memorial hall of the United Reformed Church. This was a gun room during the Napoleonic Wars. Behind the memorial hall, used to be a tannery.

Finally, to the east is St. Andrew's Church and the Clergy House. The Clergy or Priest's House dates from about 1350. It is constructed of oak framing, filled with wattle and daub. The whole being covered with a thatched roof. The interior mainly consists of a large area open to the rafters with a rammed chalk floor. It was the first building to be purchased by the National Trust in 1896 for the princely sum of £10 and is open to the public from Easter until the end of October.

St. Andrew's Church was erected about 1360. It is built in the form of a Greek cross and the materials consist of knapped flints and greensand quoins. Evidence suggests a church existed in Alfriston long before this, possibly dating back to Saxon times. As with many old buildings, churches, or places of interest, a traditional story is attached. St. Andrew's has one that goes like this.

"The church was due to be built on a stretch of land to the west of the village. The stones were put into place to form the foundations and outlines. Overnight, however, a supernatural force removed the stones and positioned them on the Tye. Somebody, then noticed four oxen lying together forming a cross. This was taken as a sign or omen that the church should be sited on that spot, which is where it stands today".

Visitors to the "Cathedral of the Downs" can purchase detailed information on the history inside the church itself.

The Tye (or village green), along with the Memorial Hall next to the church and the Gun Room, plays host to many of the village's annual events, including the Alfriston Festival. This takes place at the end of August and lasts for a week, culminating in the Bank Holiday Monday Fair. Watching the 'goings on' of the fair from a quiet corner of the churchyard will make one aware of the curious, timeless quality that pervades Alfriston throughout any event and every season.

THE CUCKMERE VALLEY

Before we start to explore however, let us muse for a minute or two on the previous inhabitants of this valley, not just one or two hundred years ago, but a few thousand years ago.

Certainly it was inhabited by prehistoric man, the findings of flint and bronze implements have been confirmed by the experts to be of the prehistoric era. So too have the earthworks and tumuli found on the surrounding downland.

As we move on through the ages of early man, much of which there is only scant evidence, we stop briefly to examine the Roman occupation, which lasted about 400 years. Although not particularly evident in this area some coins and artefacts have been unearthed by the enthusiast and the long, almost straight Roman tracks can be seen, stretching across the Downs to Firle, west of Alfriston, into the valley and up to the highest point of Windover, east of Alfriston. Here one can still trace the outlines of early Roman encampments, clinging to the hillside, giving far-reaching views of any would be marauders.

Primarily though, Alfriston is a Saxon valley. The Saxons arrived here in the 5th century and findings suggest that there were fairly large Saxon settlements within the Cuckmere valley. In 1912 a Saxon graveyard was discovered at Winton Street, between Alfriston and Berwick. About a hundred and fifty graves were excavated. Included in the graves were the personal possessions such as beads, pottery, buckles, glass bowls, spear heads and swords. Many of the exhibits can be viewed in the Anglo-Saxon room at the Barbican House Museum in Lewes. A cross was erected on the burial site shortly after its discovery.

It is interesting to think how that early Saxon influence still remains in this part of the country. Even the name 'Sussex' was derived from a word meaning 'South Saxons', and many of the villages have names ending in the Saxon suffixes of 'ing, ly, ham or ton' — such as, Alfriston, Litlington, Michelham etc. So too, is the name 'Cuckmere' from a Saxon word meaning 'flowing water'.

Did the landscape, we ask ourselves, look the same, when our distant Saxon forbears inhabited the area?

It is known there were trees and scrub covering the now relatively bare Downs. Although the beginning of clearing the forests is not directly attributed to the Saxons, it is thought that man started deforestation as far back as 3000 BC in an early attempt at cultivation and grazing. Inevitably, as the downs became bare, soil erosion happened and trees never reappeared on the East Sussex downland, instead the thin chalky soil is home for brilliant patches of yellow gorse, white hawthorn and a myriad of short stemmed downland flowers.

The River Cuckmere, we know, was a good deal wider in the 5th century. If you drive or walk to the top of Hindover, a well known beauty spot near Seaford, you can gaze at the entire, unrivalled vista of the Cuckmere valley. Here it is easy to see the width and path the river once followed.

As its Saxon name suggests, it then 'flowed' to the sea. Now it winds beautifully but idly to meet the English Channel. The cause for its idleness is due to silting up from lack of use and the need to remove obstructing shingle and soil. In early days it was a hunting or fishing ground for the communities clustered round its banks, their daily existence, as even ours is now, dependant on water. Years later barges and boats used to transport goods, and in the nineteenth century, soldiers to and from Alfriston. Then, there were the smugglers, rowing silently up the shadowy water, their ill-gotten gain stowed in the bows. All this has ceased. Now swans, herons and a motley collection of ducks claim the river as their own and the streams and marshy ground it leaves behind is a rich and fertile pasture for wildlife and plants.

1. West Street
2. The Sanctuary
3. South Downs Way

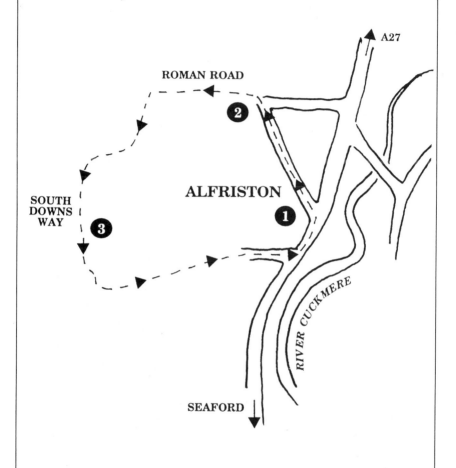

ROUTE DIRECTIONS

From the market Cross in Alfriston, take the road that leads to the north by The Smugglers Inn. This is West Street (1). At the top of the hill turn left by a house called The Sanctuary (2) built on the site of the Saxon graveyard. Turn left having reached the Downs and traverse the side of them. At the top turn left on to The South Downs Way (3). Continue for a quarter of a mile, then bear left down the hill and back into Alfriston.
Distance - Approx. 2 miles

Walk 1:
ALFRISTON, ROMAN ROAD AND THE SOUTH DOWNS WAY

A scenic walk travelling across the downland surrounding Alfriston to the south west. The route passes the site of the Saxon graveyard excavated in 1912 and heads towards the foot of the Downs by way of Roman Road, so called because our Roman ancestors had a habit of constructing unbending tracks. In late spring, look for the spiky flowers of the spotted and pyramidal orchids that bloom snugly on the sheltered grassy slopes. Contrastingly, on the hill top, splashes of yellow gorse provide vivid colour where the bridlepath joins the South Downs Way. Also, from this point are the most wonderful views across the distant rooftops of Alfriston then down the entire Cuckmere valley to the smudge of blue sea at Cuckmere Haven.

The Village Square, Alfriston

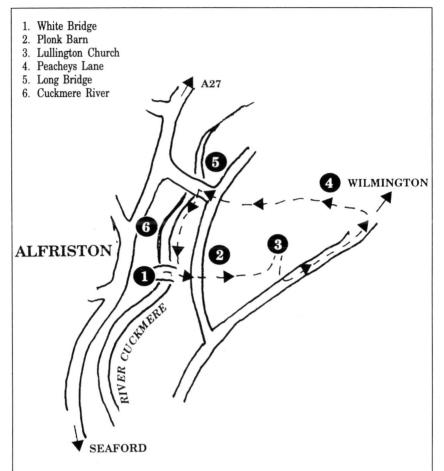

1. White Bridge
2. Plonk Barn
3. Lullington Church
4. Peacheys Lane
5. Long Bridge
6. Cuckmere River

A27

WILMINGTON

ALFRISTON

RIVER CUCKMERE

SEAFORD

ROUTE DIRECTIONS

Cross the River Cuckmere at White Bridge (1) near St. Andrew's Church in Alfriston. Follow the footpath ahead, then cross the road to a gate by the side of Plonk Barn (2), converted into an unusual home. Having passed through a second gate, continue uphill to Lullington Church (3), ignoring the footpath on the left. After visiting the church, turn left back on to the footpath and left again on reaching a road. At the top of the hill, opposite a gateway onto downland, turn left. Continue down Peacheys Lane (4). At the bottom of the lane follow the road up to Long Bridge (5). Go through the first gate adjacent to the bridge and continue by the Cuckmere River (6), until reaching White Bridge again.

Distance - Approx. 1³/₄ miles.

Walk 2:
LULLINGTON CHURCH AND LONG BRIDGE

The pretty footpath leading to Lullington Church, passes through the water meadows before climbing the gentle slope to this minuscule place of worship whose painted belfry, peeps enticingly above the trees. The atmosphere is utterly peaceful and it is easy to linger here, perhaps simply watching the sun set over the Downs. Lullington Church dates from the 13th century and is a part of a much larger church, destroyed during the time of Cromwell. All that remains is the chancel, which seats about twenty people. It was united with Alfriston in 1927 and services are held once a month.

The return route will take you via the wooded Peacheys Lane and then to Long Bridge. Evidence suggests that, during the latter part of the 18th century, the fields by Long Bridge used to be the site of a splendid roadside inn called The Royal Oak. Rather sadly, there is not a shred of evidence for the untrained eye to enjoy, so it's all left to the imagination to re-create, whilst strolling back along the towpath.

Lullington Church

1. White Bridge
2. Litlington Church
3. Frog Firle
4. Plough and Harrow

ROUTE DIRECTIONS

From White Bridge (1) take the footpath that runs between the church and the river. Go past the back of the Clergy House and Deans Place. Continue until you see the weather boarded church tower of Litlington (2) on the left. Shortly after, the hamlet of Frog Firle (3) will appear to the right. Proceed along the towpath until reaching a bridge. Turn left across it and immediately left again. The footpath to the Plough and Harrow (4) in Litlington will be on the right. Return to this point if going into the village and simply follow the eastern towpath back to Alfriston.
Distance - Approx. $2^1/2$ miles.

Walk 3:
ALFRISTON TO LITLINGTON

The river, from Alfriston to the sea at Cuckmere Haven, offers about four miles of superb towpath walking. The circular walks in this book cover most of it in easy distances. Just north of White Bridge, where this route starts, are the remains of an old wharf, mostly hidden by silt and only vaguely visible when there is a very low tide. The first person to navigate the river to this point was a John Lower, born in 1735. The last person to bring his barge here was Captain Nye, on board the 'Iona', in 1915. Today, swans, ducks, local geese and sometimes herons mill around this watery stretch instead. Recently, the swans have taken to nesting boldly amongst the rushes near the bridge, enabling onlookers to get some marvellous 'close-ups'.

Look to the west between Alfriston and Litlington and you will see the interesting properties of Frog Firle. Recorded in 1288 as 'Frogge Ferle', it is a district within the parish of Alfriston. There is the 16th century Frog Firle House, home of the Austen-Leigh family (descendants of Jane Austen) until 1950. Since then it has been used as a Youth Hostel. Tollers or Follers Manor dates from the 15th century. Place House, owned by the Chowne family for over two hundred years, was the scene of a disastrous fire in 1765. Much of it was destroyed and what was left has been re-named 'Burnt House'.

On reaching Litlington, do stop for a drink at the lovely old pub, the 'Plough and Harrow', before returning to Alfriston on the eastern side of the river.

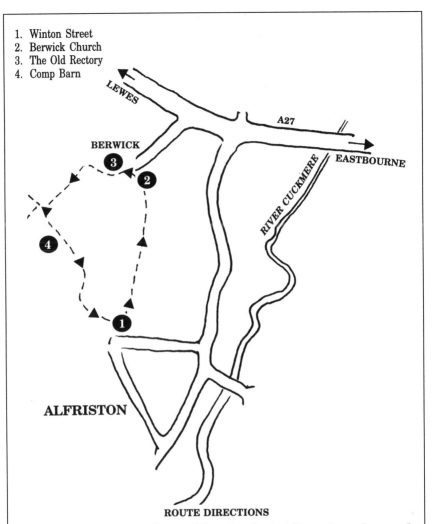

1. Winton Street
2. Berwick Church
3. The Old Rectory
4. Comp Barn

LEWES

A27

BERWICK

EASTBOURNE

RIVER CUCKMERE

ALFRISTON

ROUTE DIRECTIONS

At the top of Winton Street (1), take the bridlepath to the north and almost instantly, bear to the right, following a footpath along the edge of a field. Continuing in a straight line through the next three fields, make for Berwick Church (2), clearly visible amongst the trees ahead. After visiting the church, re-join the footpath and proceed past the walled garden, south of The Old Rectory (3). Turn left at the bottom of the slope and left again at a sharp corner towards a flint barn. This is a part of the old turnpike road and will take you past Comp Barn (4), now a private residence, back to Winton Street.
Distance - Approx. $1^3/4$ miles.

Walk 4:

WINTON STREET
TO BERWICK CHURCH

In spite of its suburban name, Winton Street is a rural lane with thatched cottages, converted flint barns and pretty gardens. The village of Berwick lies a mile or so to the north and Berwick Church, situated on rising ground, can easily be seen from the top of Winton Street, where there is also parking. Alternatively, one can park the car in Alfriston and proceed up West Street as in Walk 1.

Don't miss seeing Berwick Church. It is both delightful and unusual. The interior has been decorated with wall paintings by the famous Bloomsbury artists: Vanessa Bell, Quentin Bell and Duncan Grant, who lived nearby at Charleston Farmhouse, Firle. The imaginative work, completed in 1942 and dedicated by the Bishop in 1943, depicts various scenes, mostly with the Downs as a backdrop. The original leaded windows of the church were destroyed during the war and the introduction of clear glass panes benefits the murals by making the interior lighter and brighter. The return path from Berwick travels along the old turnpike road that ran between Lewes and Eastbourne until 1812.

Wall painting in Berwick Church

1. Deans Place Hotel
2. Bo-Peep
3. Barns
4. Cross Dyke

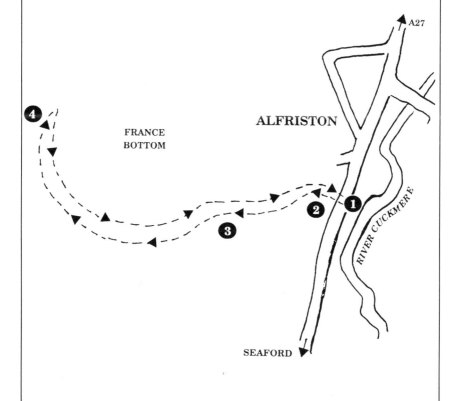

ROUTE DIRECTIONS

*At the southerly end of Alfriston, opposite Deans Place Hotel
(1), are two bridlepaths, either side of Deans Barn. Take the one
that says Bostal Bottom and Bo-Peep - 4 miles (2). Keeping to
the right, go past some tennis courts and then a few derelict
barns (3). Continue uphill for about a mile until the bridlepath
turns sharp left. This area is Cross Dyke (4). Return by the
same route.*

Distance (there and back) - Approx. 3 miles.

Walk 5:

FRANCE BOTTOM

This is not a circular walk, but one that takes you to a high view point above a large downland 'bowl'. From here you can see all the footpaths criss-crossing in every direction. It's up to you to choose where and if you'd like to extend the trail. However, do refer to the local Ordnance Survey Pathfinder map 1324 before setting off. Alternatively, it's very pleasant to follow the bridlepath up to Cross Dyke and back, just to enjoy the extensive panorama from Cuckmere Haven, Seaford and Newhaven to the sweeping vista of Firle Beacon in the west. Alfriston is completely hidden. The 'hollow or 'bowl' is called France Bottom; the name linked to the tale that during the Napoleonic era, French prisoners of war were held captive here. Today, horses and a few llamas from the local Drusillas Zoo graze in the sheltered fields.

1. Wilmington Car Park
2. The Long Man
3. The Holt

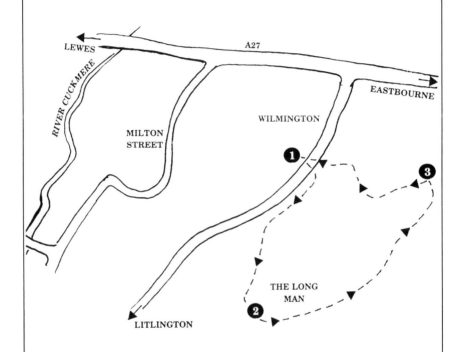

ROUTE DIRECTIONS

Cross the road from Wilmington car park (1) and turn right along the footpath. Turn left on to a bridleway and head towards the Long Man (2). After a gate at the foot of this gigantic outline, turn left and traverse the Downs north-eastwards, past a small copse. In the top right hand corner of the field, almost hidden in woodland, is a gate. Turn left after the gate on to a bridleway. This area is called The Holt (3) and used to be a part of the Lewes to Eastbourne turnpike road. Continue downhill for about three quarters of a mile, arriving back in Wilmington, opposite the church.
Distance : Approx. 2 miles.

Walk 6:

WILMINGTON
AND THE LONG MAN

The pretty village of Wilmington, tucked beneath the Downs, consists of one long lane with attractive properties, a pub, a lovely church and the remains of a 13th century priory. There are no shops; gone is the old smithy, the baker, the local school and the grocers. Only the house names give an indication of the trade that once took place within.

At the southern end of the village, lorded over by the famous chalk figure of the Long Man cut into the hillside, is a convenient car park. Close by, are the substantial remains of a 13th century Benedictine Priory, which until recently was open to the public. In the churchyard of St. Mary and St. Peter is a magnificent yew tree, thought to be a thousand years old. Its girth is so wide that it has to have massive supports under the spreading branches. Before walking to the Long Man, be sure to read the information board about him, sited near the entrance of the car park. This huge giant carved on Windover Hill has origins that still puzzle the experts. Why was he put there? Was he carved during Neolithic times? Was he carved to indicate the priory? Perhaps he was a god or maybe just a hoax? Did he originally hold a scythe and a rake? So many questions, plenty of imagination but no definite answers, yet. Meanwhile his frame is clearly outlined, the staves he holds are approximately 230 feet high and visitors flock to his form, possibly having their own theories as to why he was put there.

The Long Man, Wilmington

1. Lullington Court Farm
2. Lullington Heath and Jevington
3. Lullington Heath Nature Reserve
4. Windover Hill Viewpoint

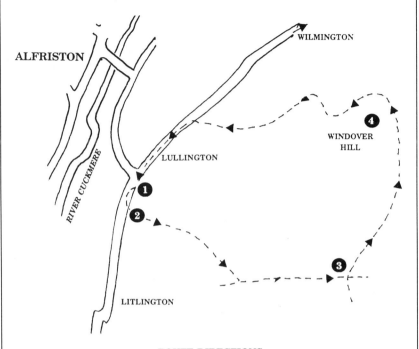

ROUTE DIRECTIONS

*The walk starts by Lullington Court Farm (1), which lies by a T-junction where the road sign indicates: Alfriston, Litlington and Wilmington. There is some parking besides a tiny quarry. Having left the car, follow the road southwards and almost immediately turn left by a bridlepath sign to Lullington Heath and Jevington (2). Follow the track uphill for about a mile, keeping to the left. Having reached a crossroads of bridlepaths and an information board on Lullington Heath Nature Reserve (3), turn left. Continue northwards passing through two gates. The track now veers slightly to the left and after half a mile is joined by a bridlepath from the right. Keeping to the left after another gate, the track then takes you past the site of the old Roman encampments and viewpoint (4). Continue to descend until reaching the road. The route is wide and easy to follow. At the road turn left back to Lullington Court Farm.
Distance - Approx. 4 miles.*

Walk 7:

LULLINGTON HEATH NATURE RESERVE AND WINDOVER HILL

If you want to see almost the entire panorama of East Sussex spread before you, then this is a walk not to be missed. Take a picnic, for you'll surely want to spend some time exploring the surrounding terrain of this four mile trek. The footpath rises very gently up the Downs from Lullington Court Farm to Lullington Heath. This nature reserve lies 152 metres above sea level and covers 62 hectares. It was established in 1954 and is one of the largest chalk heathlands remaining in Britain. The entirety is leased from the Forestry Commission who manage the adjoining Friston Forest. Wildlife is plentiful, the gorse and scrub providing a sheltered habitat for foxes, badgers and rabbits. Take care though, for in warm weather one or two adders may rest in protected spots; they are harmless enough, if left undisturbed. Midsummer brings the butterflies such as marbled whites, chalk hill blues, brimstones and the dark green fritillary. Six different species of orchid have been recorded and the birds of the open downland include skylarks, warblers, finches, kestrels and whitethroats.

From Lullington Heath the footpath veers northwards towards Windover Hill, some 700 feet above sea level. The visible mounds and bumps, on the top of Windover, indicate the workings of ancient Roman encampments. This is also the most outstanding viewpoint in East Sussex. On a clear day one can see from the High Weald to the North Downs; to the perimeters of West Sussex and the sheer cliffs of Beachy Head in the south east. Firle Beacon, Mount Caburn and Arlington Reservoir are prominent in the foreground.

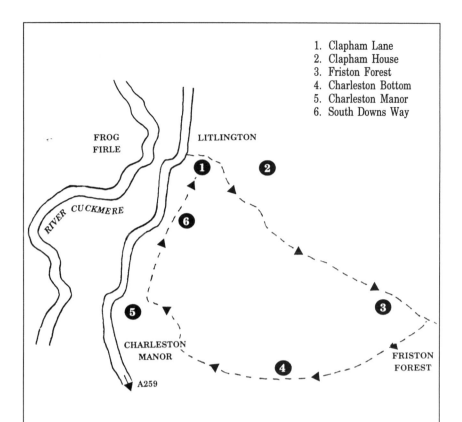

1. Clapham Lane
2. Clapham House
3. Friston Forest
4. Charleston Bottom
5. Charleston Manor
6. South Downs Way

FROG FIRLE

LITLINGTON

RIVER CUCKMERE

CHARLESTON MANOR

A259

FRISTON FOREST

ROUTE DIRECTIONS

At the southern end of Litlington, turn left up Clapham Lane (1). Follow the tarmac road until reaching the driveway to Clapham House (2) and a small cottage. Bear right. Continue uphill, past a converted flint barn on the left and then some modern working barns on the right. Proceed along the bridlepath, down a short incline (plenty of cowslips here in the spring), and carry on until reaching a gate into Friston Forest (3). A short distance after the gate will be a large clearing. Turn sharp right here and follow the footpath sign to Charleston Manor. Walk along the floor of the valley for about a mile. This is Charleston Bottom (4). At another footpath sign by the grounds of Charleston Manor (5), turn right. Turn right again at a stile and climb the hill. This is part of the South Downs Way (6) and at the top of the hill will lead directly down into Litlington. Distance - Approx. 3 miles.

Walk 8:

LITLINGTON, FRISTON FOREST AND CHARLESTON MANOR

Hidden away behind Litlington lies the handsome Clapham House; positioned amongst trees at the top of Clapham Lane, it looks across to Hindover Hill. At one time it was owned by Mrs. Fitzherbert, the mistress of George IV. Legend romantically suggests he used to gallop across the Downs from Brighton to visit her. For a number of years, Clapham House was the home of a French cookery school, but recently it was sold and is in private ownership once more.

Friston Forest extends across nearly 2000 acres of chalk downland and is a water catchment for the Eastbourne Water Company, who lease it from the Forestry Commission. There are many signed forest walks to follow, although this particular trail only touches a very small part of the woodland. Do look for the foxgloves and the pink willow herb that grow freely here in the early summer. Friston is derived from the Saxon words 'Fryers Tun', meaning - overgrown land. Apparently this area had a good deal of scrub vegetation growing in 1926, which is when planting began. The forest consists mainly of beeches, interspersed with pines, planted to provide protection for the vulnerable young beech trees. The pines are removed after about twenty years.

Having delved into Friston Forest, the trail then meanders along Charleston Bottom towards Charleston Manor. Not to be confused with Charleston Farmhouse, near Firle; the home of Vanessa Bell, sister of Virginia Woolf. This stretch of downland is an excellent habitat for badgers and foxes. Both can sometimes be seen, even in broad daylight, prowling across the short turf. Charleston manor is not large, but the outbuildings are extensive and include a magnificent barn and a clock tower. The lovely gardens, together with the barns are used for various events throughout the season and are then open to the public.

1. Plough and Harrow
2. New Bridge
3. The White Horse

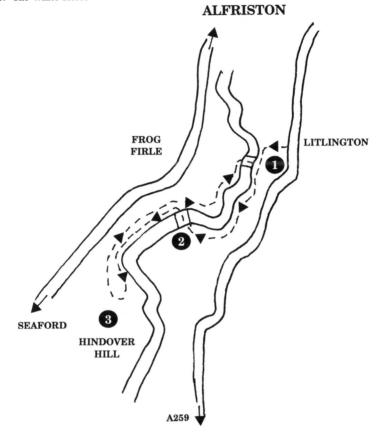

ROUTE DIRECTIONS

Follow the signed footpath to the river, just north of The Plough and Harrow (1) in Litlington. Turn left along the near side river bank and keep to the towpath until reaching the second footbridge. It's about half a mile from the village and is called New Bridge (2). Cross this and walk a short distance to the left to get a good view of the White Horse (3). The return route follows the western bank of the river until reaching the bridge and footpath into Litlington.

Distance - Approx. 1¹/₂ miles.

Walk 9:

LITLINGTON, THE RIVER AND THE WHITE HORSE

Litlington, its Saxon name meaning 'Little Homestead', appears to have stood still with time. The flint cottages clad with unruly roses, have barely changed according to one former resident. This same lady also had an amusing tale to tell. When a small boy, her father had lived opposite the Plough and Harrow in Litlington. One day he was sent to fetch a jug of ale. Dusk was falling and in his haste to get there, he tripped and fell down the well. His cries for help were heard by half the village. They ran to the scene and, unceremoniously, hauled him out, wet and cold in the well bucket. Fortunately, none the worse for his experience.

Positioned side by side, Litlington Tea Gardens and Litlington Nurseries have been a combined business since the 1930's, when they were owned by the Russell family. This 'Olde Worlde' tea gardens is still reminiscent of the Edwardian days and serves some of the best fare in Sussex. The White House, opposite the Tea Gardens, was once the Litlington Arms; subsequently it became a guest house. The church, St. Michael The Archangel, has a Norman nave and chancel, with more recent additions and it is suggested the mellow Church House Farm, beyond, could have been the Priest's House.

Walking along the river, one cannot fail to notice the White Horse, cut near the top of the steep-sided Hindover Hill. At nearly 90 feet long, it prances gaily below the ridge of the Downs towards the sea. It was carved somewhere around 1920 by a Mr. James Pagden and friends, supposedly after an evening of heavy drinking at The Smugglers Inn in Alfriston. The story suggests that, in spite of their inebriated state, the carving was completed within a few hours. The group then crept back into Alfriston, well before dawn and feigned surprise, along with the rest of the community, at its discovery. Today, The White Horse is owned by the National Trust and has been fully restored.

1. Exceat Car Park
2. Westdean Pond
3. Westdean Church

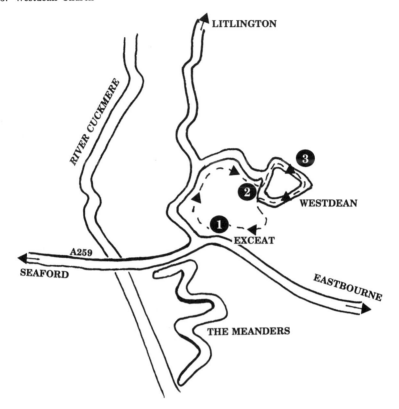

ROUTE DIRECTIONS

From the car park (1) behind the barns at Exceat, take the footpath to the north. It's signed 'Woodland Walk and Westdean'. Bear right after a short distance and continue along the edge of the forest, keeping to the left and then following the sign to Westdean only. On reaching the village pond at Westdean (2), take the lane opposite, alongside Forge Cottage, leading slightly uphill. This does a circuit of the village, passing the church (3). Having reached the pond again, turn left and climb the steps up through the trees. Please note the climb is rather steep. At the top, cross the stile by the information board (4), then continue downhill and through the gate leading into Exceat.
Distance - Approx. 1¹/₄ miles.

Walk 10:

EXCEAT AND WESTDEAN

A complex of restored barns, a farmhouse and a cottage, by the A259, make up Exceat today. Sited within the barns are three attractions. First, is The Living World Exhibition, which contains a collection of exotic and native living creatures shown in their natural settings. Next is The Seven Sisters Country Park centre. This provides full information and displays on the surrounding area. Finally, the Cuckmere Cycle Company offers bicycles of all shapes and sizes for hire at an hourly rate. In the 17th century farmhouse is a restaurant and tearooms, catering for the visitors needs, from a snack, cream tea or three course meal. Parking is to the rear of these buildings.

Initially, the footpath hugs the edge of Friston Forest, then leads into the picture postcard village of Westdean. Like Wilmington, Westdean once had farms, a blacksmith, a school and a shop. In 1801, the parish had 2000 sheep, 56 oxen and 30 horses; enough to keep several families employed. Now the barns have been converted and it has become a quiet residential hamlet, but very attractive and well worth visiting. During Saxon times, Westdean claimed royal connections; King Arthur was supposed to have his estate and hunting lodge hereabouts. One of the most outstanding properties in Westdean is the Old Parsonage; a 13th century flint dwelling, built by the monks of Wilmington Priory. The adjacent church has an unusual 'capped' tower and just around the corner are the well preserved buildings of a former farmyard. Cut into the hillside by Westdean pond is a long flight of steep steps. These will bring you onto the downland above Exceat. At this point there is an information board and the most superb vista of the River Cuckmere, its meanders and the sea.

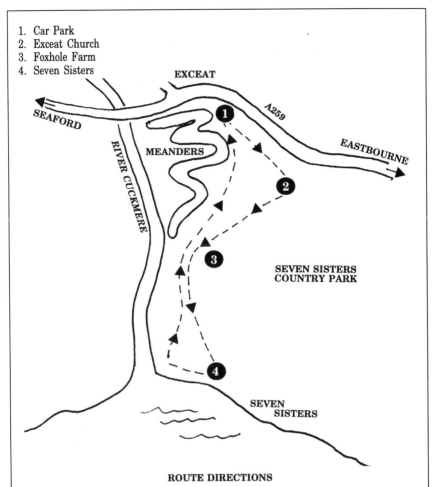

1. Car Park
2. Exceat Church
3. Foxhole Farm
4. Seven Sisters

EXCEAT

SEAFORD

A259

EASTBOURNE

RIVER CUCKMERE

MEANDERS

①

②

③

④

SEVEN SISTERS
COUNTRY PARK

SEVEN
SISTERS

ROUTE DIRECTIONS

Go through the gate from the car park (1) on the coastal side of the A259 road. Turn right, then immediately bear left and take the footpath that traverses the hill above the concrete track leading to the sea. Continue uphill until close to a fence; the memorial stone marking the site of Exceat Church (2) will be visible just ahead. Turn right at the fence, then proceed down the hill. turn left along the path leading towards the coast, passing Foxhole Farm (3) on the left. Keep to the path that travels along the foot of the downland until reaching those magnificent chalk cliffs (4) sculpted by erosion. For the return route simply follow the same footpath all the way back to the car park.
Distance - Approx. 3 miles.

Walk 11:

THE SEVEN SISTERS COUNTRY PARK

The Seven Sisters Country park covers over 700 acres and spans the lower reaches of the Cuckmere Valley and a part of the much photographed cliffs, The Seven Sisters. Here, the natural course of the River Cuckmere was to follow the meanders, which are a major feature of this area. However, in 1846, in order to reduce flooding, the river was 'canalized' or straightened, south of Exceat Bridge. Until the late 1950's, the East Sussex Transport and Trading Company operated a drag line to collect shingle for the building trade, from the beach by the river mouth. This was loaded into little dumper trucks on a tiny railway and pulled by a small engine back to the main road. There is no trace of the railway today and the loading ramps for the shingle are where the car park now stands.

Apart from being an Area of Outstanding Natural Beauty, the park is a haven for water wildlife. The shallow lagoon, near the beach, was specially constructed to enable wading birds to feed, whilst the shingle islands, mud flats and scrub provide a nesting ground for resident and migrating birds. These include: ducks, gulls, swans, herons, redshank, plovers, avocet, cormorant and grebes. The park is owned by the East Sussex County Council and managed by the Sussex Downs Conservation Board. An excellent Visitor centre is housed in the 18th century barn opposite the car park.

Before reaching the sea, the walk explores the site of Old Exceat, a Domesday village set high on the hill above the river. In 1332, the tax returns for Exceat indicated a population of nearly a hundred. Unfortunately, due to its accessibility, it was continually plundered by the French and then finally depleted by the Black Death. In 1528, when the almost ruined village had only one householder left, Exceat became united with the neighbouring hamlet of Westdean. A memorial stone marks the site of the church.

Walk 12:

CUCKMERE HAVEN

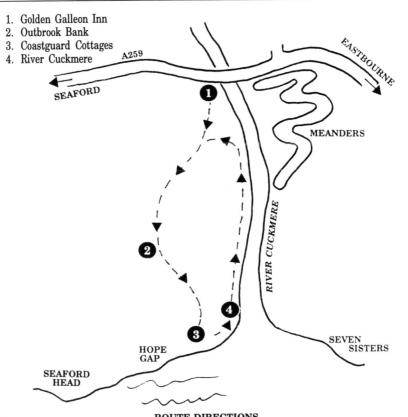

1. Golden Galleon Inn
2. Outbrook Bank
3. Coastguard Cottages
4. River Cuckmere

ROUTE DIRECTIONS

The Golden Galleon Inn (1), adjacent to Exceat Bridge, marks the start of this walk. Cross the stile in the far corner of the Galleon car park. Follow the path, cross the next stile ahead and continue directly towards the sea, ignoring a footpath to the right. The track now weaves around to follow the hills. This stretch is called Outbrook Bank (2). On reaching the coast, do explore around the old Coastguard Cottages (3), before turning left along the beach. Turn left again having reached the mouth of the River Cuckmere (4) and follow the towpath until it rejoins the last part of the route returning to the Golden Galleon.

Distance - Approx. $2^1/_2$ miles.

The western side of the River Cuckmere offers more superb walking along the cliff tops of Hope Gap and Seaford Head. Notice the old Coastguard cottages perilously perched on the edge of the cliffs at the mouth of the river. At one time there was ample ground between the cottages and the sea, but the prevailing winds have caused the waves to lash against the cliff face and the chalk has eroded at an alarming rate. It is a constant struggle to keep the sea wall shored up and in a reasonable state of repair.

Did the coastguards 'look out' deter the smuggling, which was rife in this area? Probably not, for it appears that at least half the local inhabitants were involved. Records of 1783 indicate " Two gangs of 200 or 300 carried away contraband from Cuckmere Haven, their sheer numbers overcoming the Preventative Officers. " The proximity of Sussex in relation to Europe, naturally made it an ideal place to ply such a trade. As well as goods being smuggled in, like brandy, rum, tobacco, lace and silks, goods were smuggled out. This was known as 'owling', the illegal exporting of wool; for Sussex fleeces were highly prized in Europe.

Do walk up beyond the Coastguard Cottages. Undoubtedly, this is the best spot to see the sheer cliffs of The Seven Sisters in their entirety. Many an artist has captured this scene on canvas and in all sorts of weather, too. The same panorama has also witnessed shipwrecks. In the last five hundred years, there have been at least twenty-five between Birling Gap and Cuckmere Haven.

Seven Sisters and Cuckmere Haven

The White Horse, Hindover Hill and the River Cuckmere

BEYOND THE VALLEY

The Cuckmere river does not of course finish where the Downs that form the valley part, one side to the east, the other to the west. It travels northwards past Arlington and Michelham, where it divides and becomes two mere streams. It has two sources, one at Heathfield and one at Possingworth. Both are about twenty miles from the sea at Cuckmere Haven.

Back to the busy A27, which is where this book began. Almost adjacent to the turning for Alfriston is **Drusillas Zoo Park**. Started originally by a Captain Douglas Ann during the 1930's as tearooms, the zoo has now become one of the leading family attractions in the south east. It is still run by the same family.

A beautiful place to visit is **Michelham Priory** at Upper Dicker. This outstanding 13th century Augustinian Priory is in a lovely moated setting by the river. It has some later Elizabethan additions and as well as the priory to see, there are the grounds, some fine old barns and a water mill.

Abbots Wood, near Arlington is walker's land. It is a part of Wilmington Forest and the well signed woodland walk takes you past the western shores of Wilmington Lake. It is believed the lake was used to raise fish in the 13th century to supply Michelham Priory and Battle Abbey.

Finally, I hope you have enjoyed exploring the Cuckmere Valley and I hope this book will have helped you identify some walks, some history and some of the atmosphere that is an integral part of this area.

SUMMARY OF PLACES TO VISIT

Boship Tourist Information Centre, Lower Dicker. 01323 442667

The Clergy House, Alfriston. (National Trust)   01323 870001
Open - April to end October. Daily.

Drusillas Zoo Park, Alfriston Roundabout.   01323 870234
Open - All year

The English Wine Centre, Alfriston Roundabout. 01323 870164
Open - All year

The Living World, Exceat.   01323 870100
Open - Mid March to end October. Weekends in Winter.

Seven Sisters Country Park, Exceat.   01323 870280
Open - Easter to end October.
November to Easter - weekends only.

Charleston Farmhouse, near Firle.   01323 811265
Open - April to end October - Wednesdays to Sundays.

Michelham Priory, Upper Dicker.   01323 844224
Open - March to end October.